ECOLOGIZING SOCIETY

Theory

Ben Lockwood

Brief Ecology Press

ISBN: 979-8-218-81717-6

ecological nature process theories

ideas current capitalism

theory

one bookchin first political

society production development

capitalist form dialectical human

ways social within

potential degrowth

book ecology

democratic

even

new communism

for my comrades

CONTENTS

AN INTRODUCTION

The purpose of this book is twofold. The first is to collect existing ecological theories of philosophy, politics, and economics that I feel could contribute to the formation of a more ecological society than the one we currently have in the western Global North. The second purpose is to put those theories into conversation with one another in order to identify the significant commonalities among them that provide the basis for such an ecological society.

There has never been a more pressing need to transform theory into action. We are currently, and have been for a while now, in a state of ecological and climatological crises. According to the Intergovernmental Science-Policy Platform on Biodiversity and Ecosystem Services (IPBES), both global biodiversity and the ecosystem functions it supports are deteriorating.[1] The most recent IPBES report notes that not only are these systems degrading, but that the trend is accelerating, and that goals for conserving biodiversity and ecosystem services can only be met through transforming our social and economic systems. Similarly, the Intergovernmental Panel on Climate Change (IPCC) reports that greenhouse gas emissions continue to rise, causing rapid and destabilizing changes to the atmosphere, oceans, cryosphere, and biosphere.[2] These congruent crises necessitate action guided by theories that identify the underlying causes, namely the extractive and destructive consequences of global capitalism and the structures of oppression required to sustain it.

There is a rich and highly developed body of anti-capitalist and ecological theory that can provide the foundations for such action. Thus, the first goal of this book is to collect this body of literature into a single text that illuminates the ways that each might contribute to an ecological society. In doing so, this variety of ecological theories of politics provides the foundation for a diversity of strategies linked together through their common theoretical through lines. To be clear, my goal here is not to create some new philosophy, or political ideology, or even any new practical applications. Instead, I want to pull from the variety of already-existing ideas and knowledge, finding areas of overlap among them, and areas of contrast, and combining them to produce some potential visions for what an ecological society could look like. This isn't meant to be a how-to, per se, or an instructional book, but I do want to emphasize that we already possess the information, technology, and philosophy to form the foundation of an ecological society. It's that set of knowledge that I want to aggregate into something cohesive.

Putting these theories into conversation with one another allows for the identification of important theoretical through lines. I call this collection of through lines the "nature-society thread", which permeates across these theories and links them together via the assumption that nature and society are inseparable entities.

While the nature-society thread is common to all of the theories discussed in the book, it is approachable from different directions. I call this the "bi-directionality" of the nature-society dynamic. The first direction it can approached from is that society is inseparable from nature. From this direction, I explore the theories of dialectical naturalism, social ecology, democratic municipalism, and degrowth communism. These theories are premised, to varying degrees, on the notion that society is itself an extension of the nature from which it evolved. Drawing from theorists such as Bookchin, Marx, Price, Saito, and others to show the simultaneous diversity and cohesiveness across these ideas.

The second direction one can approach the nature-society thread from is that nature is inseparable from society. From this perspective, I examine the theories of dialectical ecology, social nature, and ecosocialism. What these theories share is a critical lens through which we can examine the ways that what constitutes nature is, at least partially, a product of society itself, and that society's ideas of nature develop dialectically in relation to nature's dynamics. Here I put work from Löwy, Wallis, Castree, Braun, and Foster in contact to develop the similar critical and creative visions throughout.

Lastly, I synthesize the collective theories within the nature-society thread as varying perspectives along a theoretical continuum that arises from the dual assumptions that nature is inseparable from society, and society inseparable from nature. That neither can be fully collapsed into the other requires a holistic framework that no single theory, however broad in scope, can fully achieve.

Thus, the following series of essays, which I'm calling *Ecologizing Society: Theory* contains the theoretical background on the philosophical ideas I'm drawing from. While most radical organizing suffers from various factions forming over minor differences, the ideas upon which most radical thought is founded share in common more than they diverge. This is not to oversimplify or diminish the legitimate differences that define these separate theories, but rather to emphasize those points on which they agree, and to aggregate them along those lines into a cohesive approach.

Rather than writing for an academic audience using dense jargon, I want this book to be more widely accessible. One of the frustrations I have as an academic is that the wealth of knowledge we already possess is very rarely actually used in ways that benefit society (if it's used at all). And as Karl Marx stated, the goal is not to just interpret the world, but to change it.[3] Therefore, while I will be drawing from academic and scholarly sources, and will point these out accordingly, my intent here is to provide general audiences with information that can educate and be used to improve society, not just to contribute to abstract theoretical debates.

That said, I am of the opinion that a strong theoretical consistency is necessary to guide practical action. Without it, we too easily fall back into exploitative, oppressive, and destructive structures of society. This is why I am beginning this project with a focus on the political and economic theories which I believe are most fundamental to forming an *ecological* society. Parts two and three of this book series will focus on the methods and practices with which we might accomplish the tasks.

This book began as a series of short essays, published in my newsletter (and now press), Brief Ecology. If you've been following along, you'll recognize some of the content here. The structure is nearly identical, although I have expanded and added to the text in some areas to provide additional explanation or clarification. I very much appreciate all of those who encouraged me to write the newsletter, those who supported it in the early days, and especially those who continue to read it today. Without those readers, I never would have embarked on writing a book. So, in that context, hopefully this project proves useful in some small way.

PART ONE:

Society Is Inseparable from Nature

DIALECTICAL NATURE

As I noted previously, there are two directions from which the nature-society dynamic can be approached. The first direction I explore here is that society is inseparable from nature. The overarching premise of this book is that while nature and society are impossible to fully separate, neither can be fully dissolved into the other. This relational distinction produces theoretical divergences that can only be reconciled by examining all of its aspects.

The premise that society is inseparable from nature stems from the fact that society evolved from nature. When and where this emergence occurred is impossible locate precisely, but we know that sometime in roughly the last 200,000 years human being evolved from our previous ancestors, formed various communal groups, and these groups themselves evolved into what we might call modern society.[1] This trajectory has implications that are beyond the scope of this book, but what I want to draw attention to is that the current organizational groupings of our species, with all of our politics, culture, art, knowledge, conflicts, and cooperations originated within nature. Not only that, but we remain a part of nature, however distinctly and separately we view ourselves.[2] To draw out the conclusions of this origin, to fully understand what it means, it's important to examine the fundamental characteristics of the nature from which society emerged. Thus, the characteristic this chapter is devoted to is the dialectical aspect of nature. What we will see, shortly, is that the development of nature, or the evolution of it, has its own history. The dynamic of this historical development is the focus of this chapter.

What is Dialectics?

Before explaining what dialectical *nature* means, it will be helpful to first (as briefly as I can) provide some background on what the word "dialectical" itself means. This requires us to examine some philosophical theory, which I will attempt to summarize as quickly and easily to understand as possible. For those who are actually familiar with dialectics, I apologize for the disservice I'm about to do.

The history of dialectics is sometimes traced back to the ancient Greek philosophers of antiquity, but for our purposes a simple summary of Hegelian dialectics will be more than sufficient. In the 19th century, German philosopher, G.W.F. Hegel, developed his arguments of dialectical logic.[3] His work was focused on the form of logic, or, in other words, that ways that we understand and conceptualize the universe. For Hegel, forms of logic appear in opposing sides. These opposing sides are, for Hegel, different definitions of consciousness and the knowledge that consciousness claims to have of a given object. The contradiction in the opposing sides leads to the development of that knowledge, increasing in sophistication, nuance, and complexity. In essence, through the process of contradiction, concepts develop and subsequently generate new contradictions and new concepts, giving the formation of concepts a historical aspect. If this is abstract, it should become more concrete as we go.

Hegel identified three "moments" in the formation of a concept. These moments can be thought of as points of contradiction in the formation of concepts, where each moment comes into contact with a previous concept formation with which it contradicts. The first such moment, as Hegel defined it, is the moment of understanding, or fixity. This is when concepts originate, and seem to have a stable definition, or are fixed in the way that we conceive them. The caveat here is that the first moment is never truly the "first", because concepts do not exist in a vacuum, but rather represent a continuous development. So, this first moment is really the contradiction of previous moment, but I'll come back to that shortly. For simplicity, we can say that this first moment represents a concepts origin.

The second moment is the "dialectical" moment, or the moment of instability, when a concept becomes its negation. Here, some new idea or understanding "negates" the first moment, or, in other words, contradicts the original concept. However, this contradiction does not supplant or replace the original. For Hegel, the negation of a concept requires the initial concept to be preserved, in order for the negation to have a relational substance and contextual meaning. That is, the contradiction of the first moment is impossible without the existence of the original concept. Thus, the original concept from the first moment exists within the second.

The third and final moment of Hegel's dialectical process is the speculative moment, when the contradiction between the first and second moment is, itself, negated. Here, too, the negation preserves the original negation, or the second moment, which in turn contains the first moment, or the original concept. So, at the third and final moment, the produced concept is itself a product of the first, original concept, and the second negation of the original. In this sense Hegel's dialectic of logic is cumulative. It contains the history of its own development.

More than the "moments" of concept formation, it's the cumulative nature of Hegel's dialectical process that's most important for the idea of dialectical nature. And it's worth pointing out that Hegel himself didn't restrict his dialectics to simply individual concepts but argued that it's fundamental to our entire understanding of the universe (i.e. nature), and to nature itself. Thus, we can view nature's development, or evolution, through a dialectical framework.

How is nature dialectical?

Even though the previous explanation of Hegel's dialectics is a vast oversimplification (albeit still very abstract), it's enough for our purpose here, and I'll now turn to what should be more tangible applications of the idea. Many prominent philosophers have applied dialectics since Hegel's time, but I want to focus specifically on the work of Murray Bookchin (1921-2006).

Bookchin was a political, social, and philosophical theorist who wrote prolifically from the 1960s to the 1990s about a stunningly broad set of topics.[4] He formulated ideas about nature and society and derived a political theory from these underlying philosophies. Bookchin's work was influential across a spectrum of political circles, from anarchists to environmentalists and many other leftist areas of discourse. His theories of dialectical naturalism, social ecology, and democratic municipalism have inspired numerous academic debates and social movements both in the past and present.

Bookchin was also a somewhat controversial

figure in political and environmental circles.[5] He was an autodidact, having no formal education or training in the areas of which he wrote, published, and lectured. This meant that his method of argument sometimes differed from those conventionally used in academic discourse, and combined with his sometimes-confrontational personality, produced many strong (and often negative) opinions of him. Much more can be said about Bookchin's biography, and for a thorough explanation of his controversy's I would recommend Andy Price's book *Recovering Bookchin: Social Ecology & The Crises of Our Time.*[6] But many of these discussions are best left elsewhere. For the purpose of this chapter, I'm interested only in Bookchin's application of Hegel's dialectics to the dynamics of nature.

In applying Hegel's dialectical process to the evolutionary process. Bookchin modifies it slightly. Here, as noted earlier, Bookchin is more interested in the cumulative aspect of nature's evolution, rather than identifying moments of negation. For Bookchin, nature develops, or evolves, dialectically.[7] Every new evolutionary change occurs from a previous state. That previous state, itself, emerged from a prior state. In this way, any given ecological phenomenon is the product of its historical development. This applies to every species, population, biotic community, and ecosystem. Thus, biological evolution has a historical, cumulative aspect to it. Any current state is the embodiment of its history.

Bookchin is clear that, to him, this is a process has a direction, or a trajectory. It's not a predestined trajectory, in the sense that the universe is deterministic, but one that has a latent potential. The example Bookchin likes to give to clarify this potential is the acorn and oak tree. An acorn is not destined to become a fully mature oak; it may not germinate, it may die in infancy, be eaten by an herbivore, blow over in a storm before reaching the canopy, or any one of many possible outcomes. But we know that the acorn contains the potential to become an oak tree, because the oak tree it came from was once an acorn. The same is true for any organic entity. It's potential to exist was latent within an earlier form, otherwise it would not exist. Extend this metaphor beyond the example of individuals, to the evolution of species, and it becomes clear how nature exhibits this dialectical process.

Scale this further to an evolutionary timeline of billions of years and you gain an understanding of what Bookchin was getting at. It's a grand, philosophical vision about the nature of evolution, but lest we think this is purely a speculative philosophy, it's worth examining what the science of evolution has to offer on it. In fact, one well-established evolutionary theory appears consistent with this kind of dialectical framework. Fitness landscape theory, as it is known, is an evolutionary theory that based on quantification of a given species fitness to its environment.[8] These measures of fitness can provide information about how different phenotypes (or the observable traits of an organism) converge at the most optimal states given historical and existing development. The idea here is that while a theoretically "more fit" state for a species may exist, the species would have to become less fit, crossing a fitness landscape "valley" in order to reach a different landscape "peak", or optimized fitness. Since evolution does not produce less "fit" organisms, there is no way for this to happen unless the evolutionary pressures themselves change. And since species can only evolve from their current states, a species has to play the hand its dealt, as it were, indicating that evolutionary changes are contextual within their historical developments in ways that map well to Bookchin's dialectical naturalism.

Bookchin went on to contextualize human society within this dialectical framework of evolution. He argued that since human society evolved from a non-human nature, the potential for human consciousness and human society must therefore be latent within nature itself.[9] In other words, the material components of the nature contain the potential to develop in such a way that allows it to contemplate itself, in the form of humanity. This has some profound implications, some of which are relevant for this project.

Why does it matter?

The idea of potential leads naturally to the question of when that potential is fulfilled. Is the peregrine falcon, possibly the fastest animal on the planet, at its peak possible fitness? Is humanity's current form the fulfillment of its latent potential? On the latter question, Bookchin argued that no, it is not.[10] In fact, he went further to say that there is no such thing as a fulfillment of potential, because once a potential is realized, it suddenly becomes the latent potential of some future form. Such is the nature of a dialectical process, where the initial stage is always both the embodiment of what came before and the potential for what could come next. In this way, nature is a never-ending, evolving, and developing continuum.

This is not to say that society can't improve itself though. In fact, that was Bookchin's primary goal, to remake society in a way that fulfills its potential for democratic and ecological capacity, while simultaneously setting new potentials for itself. At the same time, Bookchin recognized a distinction between human and non-human nature. While recognizing the vast diversity of intelligence, community, cooperation, and reason that exists in non-human taxa, it was his opinion (and one that I share), that the degree to which humans exhibit these characteristics is found nowhere else in nature. Humans have a form of consciousness that is unparalleled in the rest of nature, and this, he argued, places a responsibility on us to steward, or guide, the development of nature.[11]

This is the context in which Bookchin made judgments about the current state of society. Capitalism exploits nature in order for a few people to accumulate wealth. Not only is this a domination of humanity over nature, but a domination of humans over other humans. The grotesque levels of wealth that a few individuals have attained is only possible by the exploitation of both human and non-human nature. Bookchin claims that one is not possible without the other. Thus, his view of current society is one that is grossly underdeveloped compared to its latent potential.

The foundation of his broader philosophy, which he called Social Ecology, is that society needs new ways of relating to nature, new ways of understanding our origins in nature, and new ways of relating and understanding ourselves.

Conclusion

In this first chapter, I've outlined Hegel's philosophy of dialectics and how Bookchin's dialectical nature applies it to evolutionary change. One of the primary tenets of dialectics is that it describes a process of cumulative change, of development where past states are present in current ones. As Bookchin showed, this framework illuminates the ways that all evolutionary changes occur from previous states, so that, for example, a species at a given time represents a point along a historical continuum of evolutionary development.

This also applies from the reverse view. In other words, present states existed as latent potential in previous ones, and future states are latent possibilities in our present environment. Bookchin's philosophy of social ecology, which I will cover next, is premised on this aspect of Hegel's dialectics, and applies it to both society and nature, in such a way that contextualizes society's origins within nature.

As I've laid out here, reconciling society's placement in nature has important implications for its potential future. This essay summarizes Murray Bookchin's philosophy of dialectical nature, and how he derives cumulative changes from within nature itself, dialectically. Next, I'll cover the main tenets and implications of Bookchin's Social Ecology.

THE PHILOSOPHY OF SOCIAL ECOLOGY

I've already hinted at how dialectical naturalism can be applied to society's emergence from nature. Now I want to examine that idea more directly. The theory of Social Ecology, as developed by Bookchin, extends logically from dialectical naturalism.[1] Logical consistency is a critical component to Bookchin's philosophical approach.[2] That his ideas have endured, and grown in popularity, since his death is partially due to the immensely thorough detail he gave to this logical consistency. And it is particularly evident in the way he contextualized society's origins within the evolutionary process.

As we shall see, by placing society's origins within nature one can derive an ethical framework from its ecological and evolutionary dynamics. This is based on the idea that subjectivity, in the form of human consciousness and society, arose out of the material conditions of the non-human environment. Thus, the material conditions of the environment become important metrics to evaluate the degree to which society is achieving its ethical potential. While the purpose of this chapter is to explore these ideas that are central to Social Ecology, by no means will I be able to give a full accounting of the depth of the theory. Hopefully what follows will be a suitable introduction to Bookchin's philosophy and should serve to highlight the theoretical implications that reside in the assumption that society is inseparable from nature.

Ethical Ecology

In his theory of social ecology, Bookchin argues that evolution isn't just a process of change, but that evolutionary change has a direction toward greater diversification and complexity. Many evolutionary biologists and ecologists would take issue with that statement, so it's important to emphasize what Bookchin means here. He is not referring to every single mutation, or to every change in gene frequencies at the population or community scales. Instead, he's talking about the fact that the great diversity of organic life, or biodiversity, on the planet today evolved from simple, single-celled microorganisms in Earth's history. In this sense, we can say that evolution has certainly taken a specific course toward greater diversification and more complex life forms, and even toward consciousness in the form of humanity.[3]

In fact, Bookchin actually goes further than this, arguing that the emergence of organic life from inorganic matter means that this trajectory is a fundamental aspect of the universe itself. At the time when he was writing this was a more provocative statement to make due to the lack of knowledge about our cosmos, but in light of recent findings about the potential abundance of life elsewhere in the universe, this claim has a renewed relevance and prescience. In fact, what we know about the-quite literally astronomical number of galaxies and planets in the universe lends much credibility to the notion that organic life may be a common phenomenon. Indeed, recent studies point increasingly to the probability that we will soon discover it, or perhaps already have.[4]

The possibility of a self-organizing attribute within the universe intertwines form with function, in much the same way that ecologists often study both the structure and function of an ecosystem. It also implies that organic life is a latent potentiality within matter itself. Following this line of thought leads naturally to the fact that consciousness, and society itself, is latent within matter. It's easy for these ideas to quickly spiral into metaphysical territory so abstract it verges on pointlessness. But there is a point, which is that ethical outlooks can be derived from nature itself, where diversity and complexity of both forms and functions are the necessary attributes for consciousness and society to develop.[5] Guiding nature's ecological and evolutionary development towards greater biodiversity and robust ecosystem functioning is then an ethical responsibility of humanity. Furthermore, grounding the ethical outlook within this context creates the space for value judgments on actions that do or do not align with the development of the conditions that produced human consciousness in the first place.

Our current society is increasingly aware of the harmful effects that arise from separating ourselves from nature. There is overwhelming public recognition of ongoing ecological and climatological collapse.[6] Similarly, there is a danger in equating ourselves with the rest of nature, in homogenizing and reducing all of nature's diversity into a flattened, bland oneness. To not recognize humanity's distinctness can lead to a disturbing lack of empathy for human suffering that quickly verges into misanthropy and reduces our ability to develop ethical outlooks.

As far as we know, we're the only species on the planet capable of applying a rational critique to our own ethical viewpoints, setting us apart from all other species, but, importantly, not above them. This interplay requires careful articulation of what an ecological ethics actually means, and how it can guide our interactions with our environments. This is what I want to turn to next.

Freedom, Necessity, Nature

Classical economics was founded on the idea

that nature is fundamentally scarce and insufficient to meet humanity's unlimited needs. Historically, this has led to assumptions that the structure of human society is dictated by this inherent scarcity.[7] From this perspective humanity must, by necessity, "dominate" nature in order to survive. This view has not only normalized and justified domination in general (human over human) but also paved the way for the structuring of society based on class hierarchy, competition, and exploitation. It is nearly universally accepted as a "truth" that societal hierarchy is inevitable based both on human nature and the underlying limits of nature itself. The conflict between humans reflects the conflict between society and nature. One isn't possible without the other.

To reconcile the conflict, Bookchin's Social Ecology calls for a new way of thinking, drawing out the ethical and ecological implications from the dialectical notion that society is both a part of nature, and distinct within it. Both implications stem from the diversity found in non-human nature and pre-historical humanity. New archaeological evidence is increasingly revealing a vastly under-appreciated variety of human societal structures and forms of community that reflects the biogeographic diversity from which humans emerged.[8]

Returning to this evolutionary process, Social Ecology states that evolution is a participatory process, one in which all organisms (and species) play an active role–to varying degrees–in the process of their own development. Through striving for survival, organisms participate in the evolution of their species. This participation, or "agency", is actually the precursor to what we might call human subjectivity and consciousness. Among the animal kingdom, modern humans have unsurpassed capacity to reflect upon our own development and state of consciousness, at both the individual and societal levels, and to direct it toward the ends we see fit. Thus, the participatory process of evolution produced humanity, which (so far) has in turn evolved the greatest ability to participate, and even guide, organic evolution in ourselves and other species through our actions.

Participating in our own development, and the development of other life forms, is an expression of the freedom and agency that is latent within nature. Again, because these characteristics emerged means that their potential must exist in earlier forms. That is the dialectical facet that underpins ethical and ecological development. And participating in this process in a way that enhances biodiversity and complexity will also yield greater freedom, agency, and creativity for ourselves, by definition. Participation thus becomes necessary for an ecological ethics. The people who comprise society must be self-empowered to democratically participate in determining the way society should be organized.

Following this line of thought and applying it to current society shows how far from realizing this potential we are. Current society is overwhelmingly hierarchical. Capitalism is the globally dominant economic system, where the wealth of value produced by workers is hoarded for accumulation by the ownership class. Governments exist largely to facilitate the flow of capital, regardless of the human and environmental costs. Oppression along lines of race, gender, sexuality, and disability enforce stratification within society that allow capitalism to persist.[9] All of these hierarchical structures prevent us from fully realizing our potential: A participatory, democratic, and ecological society.

Thinking Ecologically (and dialectically)

To put all of these ideas together, Social Ecology asks in what ways is society derived from nature. Social Ecology argues that society is distinct, but inseparable, from nature. The history of society's development is present in its current form, and the current form was present as latent potential in previous forms.

Thinking about ecological development in this way provides possibilities, and identifies problems, within the cumulative development of society. To take this analysis full circle, we can return to Hegel's original argument about the moments of dialectical logic and examine society from within this framework. If the original "moment" in social development was one of a diversity of forms and a variety of structures that emphasize freedom, the second or current "moment" can be viewed as one of homogenizing hierarchy. We have negated the original moment of freedom with one of oppression and exploitation.

A full reflection on this continuum, or a reconciliation of society with its origin in nature, and the ethical implications, would be a dialectical move from Hegel's second moment, to the third. We would negate the current domination of capitalist extraction and authority and return to the first moment of freedom and diversity with new insights and knowledge. This passage from society-nature into a new, speculative form, would be the first dialectical step for an ecological society, setting up new potential for us to strive to realize.

Conclusion

Bookchin's philosophy of Social Ecology is premised on the idea that organic life, consciousness, and society are all latent within inorganic matter, and thus states that these are fundamental aspects of the universe itself. Inorganic matter develops toward life, and life develops toward increasing diversity and complexity, which are the precursors to human society. In these ways, Social Ecology is an extension of dialectical naturalism.

Another core tenet of Social Ecology is that evolution is a participatory process, to varying extents across species. Human consciousness is characterized by a high degree of agency, and to participate in our own development is an expression of the freedom latent within nature. Doing so in ways that enhance our surrounding biodiversity enhances this freedom by promoting the conditions which gave rise to society in the first place. Thus, an ethical society would organize itself around the principles and conditions from which it emerged.

Combining these ideas leads to the conclusion that an ecological society is one that is democratically empowered, enabling each member of society to fully participate in how it is structured. Bookchin expresses the political element of his philosophy through what he calls Democratic Municipalism, a vision for realizing society's potential, embodying his philosophy of Social Ecology and laying out a concrete framework to guide the development of an ecological society. This is the culmination of Bookchin's ecological philosophy and is the last of this series of essays covering his work, before I move on to some other ideas about how to ecologize society.

DEMOCRATIC MUNICIPALISM

Scale is a critical feature to consider in any political and economic theory. The scale at which a theory can be implemented is as dependent on geography as it is the theory itself. Bookchin's Democratic Municipalism is a recognition of this fact in the sense that Bookchin identified the city as the most appropriate scale for politics.[1]

To understand why this is, we have to first examine what Bookchin means by "city", and also what he means by "politics", because he's using these terms in different ways than what we commonly take their meaning to be. In defining them, we identify the appropriate scale and form for Democratic Municipalism to manifest.

Doing so allows us to identify potential pathways for implementing such a system. You may remember that at the outset of this book I stated that I did not want to provide any "how-tos" to achieve an ecological society. That remains the case here. However, Bookchin did lay out a vision for how his Democratic Municipalism might take shape, while still acknowledging the need for flexibility and experimentation. I think it's worth examining his ideas around this.

Defining the City

Democratic Municipalism identifies the city (as a spatial concept) as the most meaningful and appropriate scale for actual democracy. To fully understand this requires a specific definition of what Bookchin means when he says, "the city", which he defines as an *ethical union of citizens*. For an aggregation of people living in close spatial proximity to truly become a city, they must both recognize and share an ethical responsibility to one another. The city itself must be a form of collective identity among the people that extends beyond their individual identities.

This is in total contrast to the current situation of sprawling, atomized, and alienated urban areas. Bookchin would not identify places like Los Angeles, Chicago, Toronto, Atlanta, New York, London, or Tokyo as "cities", using his definition of places where democratic politics can be realistically practiced. These places are too large in their spatial extents, too non-communal in their designs, too capitalist in their economies, and too hierarchically controlled by capital and state power. For Bookchin, a city should be a manifestation of an ecological, democratic society. It is the antithesis of our current urbanized areas.[2]

Therefore, for a city to exhibit the kind of politics Bookchin argues for, it has to be appropriately sized, adequately designed, and democratically empowered. But these characteristics can't themselves be properly identified unless we have a complete understanding of the specific politics democratic municipalism argues for.

Statecraft vs Politics

Democratic municipalism positions bottom-up politics in opposition to top-down statecraft. What we currently call "politics" in the U.S. is hierarchical control by a class of professional bureaucrats, which allow us one day of "democracy" every two to four years where we can pick new rulers–who are more or less the same as the previous ones. Whatever "revolutionary" democratic ideals remain exist only in rhetoric, having long been captured and diminished by an elite, capitalist class; something the system has been shown to be remarkably good at.[3] In contrast, Democratic Municipalism calls for a participatory politics, a form democracy that happens in person where each member of society is able to fully participate if they choose to do so.

The method for this participation is the citizen assembly.[4] Townhalls, neighborhood meetings, and community gatherings are places where members of society can come together, in person, to discuss current issues (i.e. hold hearings) and then democratically develop plans to address them (i.e. craft policies). When politics happens in person, at the appropriate scale, individuals gain a greater degree of agency in deciding the political and economic structures of their lives. This agency is the soil in which true freedom can grow.

However, in order for municipalities to realize actual democracy, they must be empowered in opposition to the nation-state. Federal and state control of cities must be reduced in order for the citizens of those cities to have meaningful control at a realistic and feasible scale.[5] This is what Bookchin means by top-down statecraft vs bottom-up politics. Either the people can democratic freedom, or the state can have oppressive control. The two cannot coexist to the same degrees.

Confederal Municipalism

The purpose of Democratic Municipalism is to organize a communalist society which is structured to meet human needs based on cooperative production and democratic decision making. Bookchin believed that many of these needs can be met with local production, and that the means of production should be citizen-owned and controlled at the scale of the municipality, rather than privately capitalist or even worker-owned.

He also realized that we live in a regionalized and globalized world. Thus, even if cities become individually empowered, there would still be a need for them to coordinate with each other. Local economies may be able to meet many needs, but to assume they could meet *all* needs, and provide society with the richness and fullness could satisfy society is to ignore reality. Much coordination would thus be needed, and could be accomplished via a "confederation of municipalities", where citizen assemblies *democratically* elect deputies whose sole authority is to coordinate trade and distribution among municipalities. Such coordination could, in turn, lead to an ecological network of democratically empowered municipalities cooperating between and among themselves to meet society's needs, deploying and developing technology that increasingly provides free time for citizens to develop themselves artistically, philosophically, intellectually, physically, and politically.

This kind of ecological, municipal network could also be operable at multiple scales–in fact, it would need to–allowing for occasionally regional coordination of economic activity, or even global action if and when the need arises. Furthermore, because the foundation of policy development is at the citizen-level, the hierarchical and exploitative interests of capital are held in check, potentially even to the extent that they whither, become irrelevant, and are unable to re-develop at all. The full confederation then becomes a community of eco-communities.

All of this is, of course, a utopian vision, even if it has some specific structure to it. So, the question is how to get from current society to a democratically municipal, and ecological one. In some ways, this is the wrong way to look at it, because Bookchin argues that Democratic Municipalism is as much a never-ending process as it is a framework. Cities would dialectically develop, realizing their potentials as they simultaneously lay the seeds for future ones. But, given that this is meant to be the actualization of Bookchin's philosophy, he does provide some preliminary ideas of how society might move in that direction.

How To Get There

Bookchin saw the move toward a democratically municipal society as a long-term transition. One of the first steps he suggests is for people to simply start holding neighborhood meetings in their communities, recognizing that at first these meeting assemblies would be limited to simply discussing relevant issues. But simply getting community members into a room together to talk, and organizing regular meetings, is the most critical part of the process.

The next step would be to elect town and city councilors who advance the issues of these neighborhood assemblies. This would empower and legitimize the assemblies, encouraging more people to attend and participate in them. A feedback loop then develops, where the townhalls and assemblies become the site at which local politics are practices. Repeating this process would then further strengthen the assemblies as methods of citizen-powered, democratic control over the city or town.

Of course, this would eventually result in direct confrontations with capital and state power. Bookchin suggests the establishment of civic banks as financial institutions that could purchase and fund municipally controlled lands and other means of production. This accomplishes two goals at once. First, the banks free the city from dependence on capital investment and state-sponsored funding. As they grow, more land and infrastructure can be bought and repurposed for the benefit of the community. These institutions can then be used to meet the community's needs within ecologically oriented, democratically controlled networks.

This entire process would repeat continually, as new challenges arise, and are then met and addressed. It would also function as an educational process, whereby members of society become increasingly aware of their own ability to shape the structure of society, gain freedom in their daily lives, and an ecologically oriented agency. Thus, society develops dialectically, realizing and creating new potential in an ongoing, developmental process.

This is the full culmination of Dialectical Naturalism and Social Ecology. If we examine the theory broadly, it's clear that the implementation of Democratic Municipalism requires society to overcome the logics of capitalism. Such new forms of society would, by necessity, be fully democratic in nature. And these two characteristics pave the way for restructuring economic production to make it actually sustainable and decarbonized, which Bookchin very clearly saw as necessary to improving and developing human society.

Conclusion

Including this one, the first three essays of this series provide an overview of Murray Bookchin's theories of Social Ecology. I wanted to start with Bookchin's ideas because I think they lay a solid foundation on which any socially ecological vision for society could be grounded, because that is specifically what Bookchin's theory was designed for. What Bookchin did so well was to develop a completely consistent philosophy that locates society's emergence from within nature, and from this he derived an ethical framework for how to structure society.

To summarize, the theory of Social Ecology is founded on the principle of Dialectical Naturalism, which argues that the because of the cumulative development of evolution, we can say that the potential for society is innate within the nature itself. Social Ecology then builds on this principle, in the form that society should be structured in a way that reflects its origins in nature and promotes the environmental conditions which gave rise to society. Democratic Municipalism, is then, an example of how such a society could be structured based on participatory democracy, resource sharing, and cooperative, municipally owned forms of production.

Bookchin's theory is only one example, though, and there are many other ideas that bring together socialist and ecological concepts. The one I want to discuss next is appropriately named, Degrowth Communism. These ideas overlap and build upon Bookchin's in ways that I think lead naturally to this discussion, which I will highlight throughout.

DEGROWTH COMMUNISM

In the broadest sense, degrowth is about decelerating, or slowing down, economic growth. As more people recognize the ecological, climatological, and ethical consequences of pursuing unlimited growth, more are turning to ideas about degrowth as a potential solution. Given this rise in popularity, it's no surprise that there are many different opinions about how best to achieve degrowth. Here, I will be drawing primarily from Dr. Kōhei Saito's writing on Degrowth Communism, along with various other sources.

Saitō is an assistant professor of philosophy at the University of Tokyo. Much of his work grounds his ideas in Marx's unpublished writing, making the argument that Marx became aware of the limits to economic growth later in life and argued for a more sustainable socialism, rather than a productivist one he seemed to endorse in *Capital*.[1] While taking this approach provides a theoretical consistency for Saitō to place his Degrowth Communism squarely within the traditionally Marxist communist framework, much of his arguments are more academically oriented than is relevant here.[2] I will, however, return to the idea of Marx's contributions to ecological thought in the next chapter. For now, though, I'm going to focus more specifically on what Degrowth Communism actually is, rather than Marx's ideas that might underpin it.[3]

The Ecology-Climate-Capitalism Problem

The environmental destruction of capitalist economies is well-established, but those of us in the Global North rarely see its full extent because imperialist capitalism externalizes these harms to the Global South.[4] Rainforests are cut down to plant cash crops solely for export. Exploitative mining uses cheap labor from less wealthy nations, then destroys their environments and extracts their resources. Polluting manufacturing is moved to move vulnerable areas to make goods bought and sold in wealthy countries.[5] And climate change exacerbates all of these inequalities amid the ongoing destruction of critical ecosystems. Put simply, the lifestyles of those of us in the Global North–and more particularly, the wealthiest of us– depends on the exploitation of both labor and land in the Global South.

The problem isn't only in the Global South, though. Even within wealthy nations, growth cannot be decoupled from carbon emissions until economic production is fully decarbonized (which may not actually ever happen entirely).[6] This means that the manufacturing of renewable energy produces greenhouse gas emissions, which presents a dilemma, *since we need renewable energy in order to decarbonize.* The upshot is that in order to reduce total emissions while we transition the energy sector, other harmful and unnecessary production (e.g. fossil fuel industry, marketing, military industrialism, fast food, etc.) needs to shrink, or "degrow".

Unfortunately, capitalism provides no mechanism for this. The only way for a capitalist economy to shrink is for a financial crisis to occur. We saw this clearly in the CO_2 emissions drop during the COVID-19 pandemic, and other previous crises.[7] Considering the amount of human suffering these events produce, neither financial crises nor disease outbreaks are reasonable ways to achieve degrowth, so something else is needed. Enter: degrowth communism.

The Degrowth Communism Solution

Many environmental movements are about changing our consumption. This includes things like reusable grocery bags, recycling, buying from "sustainable" sources, and so on. But we know capitalism is not sustainable. To keep the system going, we need to keep buying more and more of these goods, even though their entire premise is to *reduce* our waste.

33

The concept is paradoxical, because capitalism requires the growth that uses resources and creates waste. Our consumption habits surely do need to change, but we can't do this and maintain capitalism at the same time.

The solution then, must be at the site of *production*, rather than consumption. In other words, we must change the way we produce the goods and services required by society. This is the foundational premise of Degrowth Communism. Guiding this kind of economy requires a framework on which production should be based. To this end, Saitō outlines five "pillars", or tenets of Degrowth Communism:

1. The first is the economy should be based on production for **use-value**. Under capitalism, goods are produced purely for exchange value, meaning that the actual use of a good or service is irrelevant so long as it generates a profit. Under degrowth communism, the point would be to prioritize the production of goods and services that have the most use and importance to society.

2. The second pillar is the **shortening of work hours**. Because wasteful, useless production would be dramatically reduced, so too would the number of working hours we have to put in. Existing (and new) technology would be leveraged to meet society's needs with less labor time, rather than squeezing more and more efficiency and production out of exploited workers. All of this means we could work much less.

3. The third tenet of Degrowth Communism is **abolishing the generalized division of labor**. Changing the very nature of work is critical to make

it a creative, attractive endeavor rather than mere toil. The division of labor standardizes, uniforms, and monotonizes work, while removing agency and creativity from workers. While some division is likely necessary and should be retained, a balance must be struck between efficiency and autonomy, in a system that provides lifelong vocational training to those who want it.

4. The fourth pillar is **democratizing production**. Giving workers decision-making power over production allows them to prioritize their own working conditions. Expanding this democratic control to the community gives society the ability to decide what gets produced and how much of it. No longer would capitalist owners be able to control and exploit workers for their own gain.

5. Lastly, the fifth tenet of Saitō's Degrowth Communism is **prioritizing essential work**. Some types of work are impossible to automate, and difficult to profit from. Jobs in care work, healthcare, and education are vital to a functioning society, but are often understaffed and underpaid in capitalist economies. A key aspect of degrowth communism is to prioritize this work by giving workers the adequate resources and pay they need to carry it out.

What Degrowth Communism Looks Like

Guiding degrowth communism by these five pillars sets it in stark contrast to the organization of a capitalist economy. Furthermore, it provides a structure by which degrowth of the economy can be equitable and democratically achieved. What the pillars don't provide, though, is a concrete vision of what degrowth communism looks like when practiced.

Luckily, Saitō identifies some examples. The "Fearless Cities" concept is one such example, which originated in Barcelona.[8] Specific policy implementations included things like reducing greenhouse gas emissions, adding public greenspace, reducing vehicular and air transportation while increasing public transportation, and promoting waste reduction. Since its inception, the network has grown to include more than 70 municipal movements.[9]

More generally, Saitō points to workers co-ops as a way to re-organize production to bring it in line with the tenets outlined above. Worker co-ops operative as collectives which are owned by the workers and/or the communities, rather than private capitalist shareholders. This gives them the freedom to operate democratically, prioritizing working conditions while meeting society's needs, without resorting to endless growth and profit-seeking.

I'll cover both of these ideas in-depth in the future, but for now it's worth pointing out that what these examples share is an emphasis on horizontality, rather than top-down authority, and a basis in local communities. If this sounds similar to the theory of Democratic Municipalism I covered previously, that's because it is. In fact, I'd argue that what Saitō is calling for is virtually identical to the kind of socially ecological organization that Murray Bookchin also argued for.

What links all of these ideas together is what Saitō calls the "revolutionary trinity". The goals of any re-organization around climatological and ecological alignment must include overcoming capitalism, reforming democracy, and decarbonizing society. And because these principals apply so aptly to both Degrowth Communism and Democratic Municipalism, I want to point the relevancy of them to this entire project. In fact, in my opinion, these three linkages apply equally well to all of the theories I discuss in this text, including the ones to come. They are the foundations on which I believe any ecological society should be based.

Conclusion

As we've now seen, Degrowth Communism is a more explicit framework for Degrowth in general. While both argue for shrinking the economy, Degrowth Communism approaches this from a planned perspective with an emphasis on tenets that put it in direct opposition to a capitalist system.

In making his case for Degrowth Communism, Kohei Saito outlines five such tenets, or "pillars", of the theory. These pillars include: 1) Use-value based; 2) Short working hours; 3) Reduced divisions of labor; 4) Democratized production; and 5) Essential work prioritized. These five tenets structure economic activity around benefiting the whole of society rather than accumulating wealth for the few.

Linking Degrowth Communism to more revolutionary politics, Saito also outlines three principles of the theory that I feel overlap well with other political theories discussed in this series. These include overcoming capitalism, reforming democracy, and decarbonizing society. Here, we can say that following the nature-society thread from the direction that society is inseparable from nature has led to two political theories that share three fundamental principles. What I will do now in the second half of this text is approach the nature-society thread from the opposite direction, that nature is inseparable from society, to show that following it from here leads to the same conclusion.

PART TWO:

Nature is Inseparable from Society

DIALECTICAL ECOLOGY

The second direction from which the nature-society thread can be approached is that nature is inseparable from society. Given that human survival is dependent on non-human nature, our interventions into nature are, to some extent, inevitable. However, the form that those interventions take can either exploit or enhance nature's inherent tendencies. Here, I want to examine the ways in which society interacts with non-human nature to identify the structural characteristics of those interactions that contribute to our current environmental crises. In doing so, we can also identify structural interactions that would ameliorate those crises and even advance the wellbeing of both society and nature.

In John Bellamy Foster's book, *The Dialectics of Ecology*, Foster traces the development of ecological thinking to the scientific socialism and materialism of Marx and Engels.[1] In their time, both thinkers recognized the destructive nature of capitalism.[2] While Engels explicitly argued for a dialectical view of the naturalism of their time, Marx developed these ideas within his pre-existing theory of economics, characterizing the environmental destruction wrought by capitalism as a rift in the mediation that labor plays between society and nature.

By placing their ideas of nature within a broader theory of dialectical materialism, Marx and Engels unknowingly contributed to the emergence of much broader ecological ideas. Many of the concepts we have today, like the ecosystem itself, originate in the application of dialectics to ecological and evolutionary phenomena. Furthermore, these ideas gave rise to the entire notion of an ecological civilization, as one in which Marx's metabolic rift between nature and society has been reconciled and the nature-society relationship harmonized.

The Social Metabolism & The Metabolic Rift

Much of the concept of a Marxist (or dialectical) ecology originates in Marx's notion of the social metabolism and metabolic rift. To fully understand the social metabolism, it's important to first understand what Marx means by "metabolism" in general. Here, metabolism refers to the full set of both organic and inorganic processes of nature.[3] This includes things like nutrient cycling, carbon storage and flux, evapotranspiration, seasonal phenology, precipitation, temperature, and so on. Of course, Marx in his time couldn't be as aware of some of the specifics of such processes as we are today, but he was very much aware of the motion of matter and energy throughout natural systems, and the levels of organization that life can be categorized into.[4] In this way, Marx's universal metabolism of nature represents what we might think of as a combination of ecosystem and community ecology.

Marx then developed his theory of a social metabolism based on this universal metabolism. Here, the social metabolism refers to the "mediation" of the universal metabolism of nature through society's activity of labor and production. The ways that society produces the goods needed to sustain itself, using the material provided by non-human nature, is the social metabolism. This refers to the specific methods labor uses to say, harvest timber or catch fish, but more importantly it refers to the structural systems that govern those methods. Marx was focused on the ways that capitalism, specifically, incentivizes methods and magnitudes of extraction that overexploit the natural world.

This overexploitation is Marx's metabolic rift.[5] The rift represents the conflict between the universal metabolism of nature and the social metabolism of society. The constant growth of capitalism requires more resources than nature itself can provide. Marx (and Engels) saw firsthand the way that capitalist agriculture stripped soil of its nutrients, and the extreme degree to which capitalist industry polluted the air of cities.[6]

While Marx and Engels didn't have our concept of sustainability available to them at the time, they nonetheless recognized the unsustainable nature of capitalism. An economic system that requires constant expansion destroys the conditions that humans rely on to survive. In short, it destroys human habitability. This is what Marx and Engles recognized, and together they applied their ideas of nature and ecology to every environmental issue of their time, including: soil degradation, deforestation, disease and epidemics, air and water pollution, animal cruelty, and regional climate change. These ideas paved the way for broader ecological thinking and had a strong influence on the development of ecology as a discipline.

Ecological Dialectics

While Marx's metabolic rift undoubtedly played a role in the advancement of ecological ideas, Engels arguably had a more direct impact. Within his dialectics of nature, Engels argues that our knowledge of nature does not simply consist of that which is external to us, but also a product of our own active engagement with external nature. This is a more developed way of saying that nature is inseparable from society, but it nevertheless returns us to that concept.

There is a deeper dialectical implication here, though. Both Engels and Marx grounded their dialectical materialism in the idea that nature itself is contingent, or contextually dependent, on past events. This is, of course, an application of the Hegelian dialectic to nature and evolution, as I discussed earlier in Bookchin's work. To reiterate, nature develops (i.e. evolves) from prior states and forms. This isn't a deterministic process, but one with specific contexts-based on the past-which constrain but do not determine evolutionary trajectories.

Adding a layer to this process is the fact that ecological thought (any thought really) develops dialectically in a very similar fashion. We can trace many of our current ecological concepts to the ideas that Marx and Engels themselves were working on. Foster's *The Dialectics of Ecology* outlines several of the ecological advancements that were influenced by their work, particularly that of Engles. These include discoveries about the link between production and disease spread, the materialist origins of life, and perhaps most relevantly the ecosystem concept put forth by noted British ecologist Arthur G. Tansley. Even more modern ecologists-such as the Marxist biologist Richard Levins, and evolutionary biologists Richard Lewontin and Stephen J. Gould-were strongly influenced by the progression of ecological work stemming from Marx and Engels.[7]

Much of this trajectory was in response to the reductionist and deterministic ideas about ecology and evolution that were arising at this time (and are also still prevalent today). Debates about whether nature can be reduced to the mechanics of physics, or whether unique properties emerge at greater levels of organization defined the discipline of ecology throughout the latter half of the 20th century.[8] Many of these debates have not been fully reconciled, and there is now a growing recognition that doing so requires stepping outside of debate itself, and adopting a contextual view of nature.[9] This view is, essentially, a return to Engels's dialectics of nature in which he outlined his three principals: 1) the transformation of quality into quantity (new forms at different levels of organization); 2) the unity of opposites between and among levels of organization; and 3) the emergence of patterns and properties as a result of the these contradictions.[10] If this sounds familiar, it's almost exactly the same framework I discussed in Bookchin's dialectical naturalism.

Ecological Civilization

The dual threads of the metabolic rift of capitalism and the dialectics of ecology provide a framework with which we can address the alienation of society from nature. Capitalism, which is based on the production of nature for the purposes of exchange-value (the value that goods can be exchanged for on the market), creates a structural necessity to exploit nature (and labor) to the fullest extent.[11] The necessity arises from the dynamics of competition and private ownership combined with a mechanism for individual wealth accumulation. These structures of capitalism pave the way for our extractive relationship to the non-human world that is currently wrecking the climate and ecosphere as a whole.

Addressing environmental destruction is to, by definition, create an ecological civilization. Returning to the Marxist tradition, in *Capitalism in the Anthropocene: Ecological Ruin or Ecological Revolution*, Foster outlines what it will take to do so, which requires overcoming the logics of capitalism. In the broadest sense, this means abandoning economic growth. But lest our opponents run amok with that claim, this does not mean abandoning planned economic development, which I will return to shortly. What it does mean is the elimination of capital. Individual wealth accumulation occurs at the expense of public wealth. The two cannot coexist.

Foster's ecological civilization also shifts production to focus on use-value rather than exchange-value. The vast quantities of resources capitalism wastes by producing goods that have no benefit to society or worse, are even harmful, greatly contribute to our climatological and ecological crises. Not to even mention the amount of goods that are destroyed because they never sold. The most immediate change would be to cut spending on things like fossil fuel use, private jets, SUVs, and the ownership of multiple homes. These luxuries of the ultra-wealthy disproportionately harm society and thus have no place in Foster's ecological civilization.

Both Marx and Engels recognized that any

socialist society that might resemble what we consider to be ecological would require a degree of planning. For Marx, planning was the mediator between collective production and individual consumption, much in the way that labor mediates between nature and society. Engels saw the role of central planning in more directly environmental contexts, particularly in addressing the ways that capitalism externalizes ecological destruction via the spatial separation between production and consumption.

In the 20th century, the Soviet Union was the first major attempt at implementing central planning. An assessment of the Soviet Union's success and failures is neither needed here nor within the scope of this project, but it suffices to say that it had a wide variety of both. In the 21st century, China is the preeminent example, and again, the degree to which China's economy is socialist or an authoritative state capitalist one is beyond this book. Though it is worth pointing out that the Chinese economy is rapidly decarbonizing despite rapid growth.[12] What these examples highlight is that for central planning to be truly socialist and ecological it must also be democratic.

Conclusion

Taken as a whole, Foster's ecological civilization strongly resembles Saito's Degrowth Communism, sharing a foundation in Marxist thought as well as the principals of an ecological society, namely overcoming capitalism, decarbonizing production, and reforming democracy. And while Bookchin's democratic municipalism is grounded in the anarchist tradition, rather than Marxist, it nonetheless shares these same characteristics.

More broadly, in *The Dialectics of Ecology* Foster reveals the degree to which the dialectics of Marx and Engles's theories influenced the development of ecological thought in the 19th, 20th, and even 21st centuries. Both quantitative and qualitative theories of ecology and evolution draw upon dialectical notions of contextual change that is contingent on prior states. In fact, it's increasingly clear that a dialectical theory of ecological phenomena is the only thing that can reconcile ongoing debates.

Dialectical Ecology also clarifies the inseparability of nature from society. Our knowledge of nature originates in our engagement with it. Our active role of participation in nature via our labor, science, philosophy, and other forms of reason contribute as much to our understanding of nature as does any of its external, non-human conditions and characteristics. This has substantial implications, which I now turn to more specifically in the next chapter.

SOCIAL NATURE

At its most fundamental level, Social Nature is premised on a single question: What is nature? This question forces us to confront the often-uncritical assumptions we make about nature, as well as who those assumptions benefit, and what impacts they have. Social nature theory begins with this question because the fact that the question is possible implies that the answer differs to different people, different communities, and different societies. In this way, nature is social, in the sense that it is socially defined.

This is not to say that there aren't common ways in which we tend to use the word "nature". In *Social Nature: Theory, Practice, and Politics*, geographers Noel Castree and Bruce Braun identify three of these common usages. The first is that we often refer to an external to society nature, or that which is non-human (e.g. trees, birds, mountains, etc.), assuming a nature-society duality. The second is an intrinsic nature, usually referring to an aspect that is internal to something (think claims on what constitutes "human nature"). The last is a generalizing, or universal nature. Here, nature is everything, the universe itself.

Within all three common usages are several

underlying assumptions:

1. **Nature is knowable:** By far the most common assumption in society is that nature is knowable. That we can-through observation, testing, and refining our ideas-determine concrete facts about how nature works which are not subject to our own biases. Social nature challenges this assumption by arguing that all "facts" about nature are interpreted through the social contexts of our time and place.

2. **Nature contains unchangeable properties:** This assumption is that nature is a solid, static entity that can't be altered at its fundamental levels. Lead can't be turned into gold, as it were.

3. **Nature lends to value judgments:** Here, nature is subject to value judgments. An example is the notion that protecting aspects of the environment is inherently good. Or that not using natural resources to the fullest extent is inherently bad. These are value judgments we place on the natural world.

The *Social Nature* text referenced above is a collection of articles by multiple geographers approaching different aspects of just how society constructs nature. While not a theory exclusive to geography, social nature is perhaps most often engaged with by geographers, given that the discipline is itself a study of people and their environments, or nature and society. According to Castree, there are two axioms to a geographic theory of social nature: 1) Nature has never been nonsocial; and 2) To view nature as nonsocial perpetuates existing oppression and inequalities.

I'll examine these axioms more closely shortly, but first it's worth spending some time on what exactly it means to know and construct nature. I think this will help clarify what the theory of Social Nature is about, before adding more depth.

Knowing and Constructing Nature

Social nature theory posits that our knowledge of nature is, at least partially, socially constructed. But what exactly does that mean? Castree examines three modes by which nature is social, and these correspond well with the assumptions outlined above, so I'll take them in order:

1. **Knowing nature:** The argument here is that knowledge of nature contains the biases and subjectiveness of the "knower". The knowledge that society produces about nature is inseparable from the cultural, political, economic, and religious characteristics of a given society. Thus, there is no single, wholly "objective" version of nature, since all knowledge of it is filtered through our societal precepts. Examples of this include racist ideas about the superiority of Caucasian people over non-Western people, gendered discrimination in multiple forms (such as the gendering of nature as feminine and needing protection that preserves patriarchic hierarchies, as well as assumptions about gender and sexuality in non-human nature), and social Darwinist claims that underpin violent, eugenicist ideas. We can

see these clearly in the anti-vaccine agenda of the current United States Secretary of Health and Human Services, Robert F. Kennedy Jr.

2. **Engaging nature:** Knowledge is not the only way we relate to nature. Practically speaking, we are almost always engaging in nature's physical aspects in some way. The forms those interactions take on is also structured by political, cultural, and other societal factors. For instance, in places like the U.S., U.K. and most of Europe, wealthy lifestyles consume far more resources than in less wealthy places on the planet and export the environmental consequences of that consumption to those same less wealthy people. Even something like famine, which we assume to be the result of environmental catastrophe like drought, has a social component in that there is virtually always enough food to feed the planet, but capitalism prevents an equitable distribution of it

3. **Remaking nature:** It's easy enough to understand the social dynamics of how we engage with nature but arguing that we remake nature itself is a direct challenge to the assumption that nature is, fundamentally, unchangeable. However, there are many examples that it isn't. Climate change is perhaps the most prominent instance of us unintentionally altering aspects of nature previously thought to be static. Within the past several decades we've seen more serious considerations of intentionally altering the planet's climate, via geoengineering, with the goal to reverse climate change. This is not to mention controversies around vaccines (I am not a vaccine

skeptic, for the record), genetically modified organisms in agriculture, and even the ability to now turn lead into gold.[2] Nature is malleable to us, and in fact always has been. Of course, latent within each of these examples is value judgment arguments about the extent to which we should alter nature.

Social Nature theory is not without its criticisms, however. The first is one I've already pointed out, that social nature directly challenges the self-evidence of the physical world around us. It implies that we cannot trust our senses and mind to accurately interpret our environments. It's not hard to see why many take issue with that kind of statement. Another criticism is that it challenges the authority of science. If we can't objectively know the world, how can we objectively study it? Both conservative and progressive political entities argue against this viewpoint and also deploy it against views with which they disagree. The last common critique is that social nature theory equates to moral relativism. If there is no objectiveness, there's only subjectiveness. Any stance on any issue is equally justifiable. All of these are, to some extent, legitimate critiques, and to make sense of how social nature adherents respond to them we need to return to the two axioms I mentioned earlier.

The first axiom was that nature has never been nonsocial. This corresponds to a particular usage of philosophically oriented social nature arguments. These are often abstract, theoretical debates about the limits of human knowledge, and what knowledge actually represents. The second axiom was that to view nature as nonsocial perpetuates existing oppression and inequalities. This is a much more specific argument about the political dynamics of how we define nature. Such positions often do not generalize about the whole of nature being socially constructed but rather examine the specific aspects of individual examples. In this way, we can say that there are two kinds of social nature; one is philosophical, and one is political.

Capitalism and the Production of Nature

Lastly, I'd like to put these concepts into the more specific context of our current, capitalist society. With examples like genetic and geo-engineering, we've already seen that nature is alterable. If we accept the social construction of concepts of nature, it opens up space for the conclusion that nature is created or produced. Again, we can point to things like genetically engineered organisms as examples of creating new natures, but even before the invention of those technologies we were creating hybrid organisms.

In the development of industrial agriculture, scientists were able to create hybrid strands of various crops that produced greater yields and were, more importantly, sterile. This meant that farmers suddenly had to buy new seeds every year, instead of cultivating their own strains, thus paving the way for capitalist control over the agricultural sector, which the incorporation of more explicitly GMOs continues today. The science that made this possible was developed at universities and research institutions like the USDA, funded with taxpayer dollars, and ultimately funneled into capitalist frameworks to extract profit.

What this example shows us is that social nature theory provides a method with which we can ask what forces drive the production of nature, and what effects that production has. Under capitalism, the accumulation of wealth via profit is the sole driver of production, very much including the production of nature. And we've seen the effects of this. Capitalist production has caused a rapidly warming planet and destabilized climate, widespread environmental destruction, and dangerous levels of pollution.

What would production look like if driven by different forces? That is up to us. I've already explored ideas like Democratic Municipalism, Degrowth Communism, and an ecological civilization based in Dialectical Ecology. The underlying question any system of production has to answer is: To what extent is it right for us to produce nature? The very ability to ask this question requires a system other than capitalism, which places no ethical, moral, cultural, or political limits on production.

The final aspect of the production of nature is to turn the concept back in on itself, in what we can call the production of social nature. Here, we not only create new forms of nature, but also new concepts of nature. And in a form of dialectical development, new concepts of nature become new forms of nature in and of themselves. One example of this is illuminated by environmental historian, Jason W. Moore, who writes about the ways that maps and satellite imagery radically re-ordered reality and made the planet conceivable in a way never before possible.[3] These maps and images thus become productions of social nature that create new natures in and of themselves.

Extending this concept, we can argue that if nature itself is a form of fiction, then forms of fiction are also forms of nature.

Conclusion

There's a lot to wrestle with within the theory of Social Nature. At its most basic conception, the theory gives us a foundation from which to ask who defines what nature is, who produces that nature, who benefits from that production, and who bears the costs. It's fundamentally a critical theory, in the sense that if nature is, at least partially, socially constructed and produced, we should be constantly critical of that process.

ECOSOCIALISM

Thus far, I've prefaced each political and economic theory with the reasons why such theory is needed. Global capitalism is wreaking havoc on our ecosphere, to the extent that the functioning of our society, the continuation of civilization, and the very existence of our species is at risk in the coming centuries. These are all the reasons why Ecosocialism is a relevant political theory for discussion. But Ecosocialism also justifies itself along another line. Socialism must be ecological.

Why Ecosocialism?

This might seem like an unusual question to begin with, before defining what Ecosocialism actually is, but the point is that the theory can only really be understood in the context of what it's in opposition to. So that's where I want to start.

The theory of Ecosocialism developed in part as a response to previous attempts of socialism (particularly the Soviet Union, as briefly discussed earlier) which emphasized production at the expense of their natural environments. In the case of the Soviets, this was largely to compete with capitalism on the global stage, and we see a similar process playing out in China.[1] That's a vast oversimplification of history, but it is nevertheless the case that many socialist states have shifted heavily toward a productivism that historically increased resource use and environmental degradation.[2]

Of more importance, though, is the current global domination of capitalism and its corresponding destruction and extraction. Capitalism is an extremely wasteful economic system. A large portion of production is undertaken solely to benefit the capitalist, ownership class, and has no benefit to society whatsoever.

Advertising is a perfect example of this. A 2018 study found that 10% of emissions produced from global internet usage were attributable to online ads alone. Digital advertising has only increased since then and now invades virtually every aspect of the online experience. Social media, which once held the promise of connecting and empowering the world, now exists solely as platforms on which companies bombard potential "customers", trying to manipulate us into giving them our money. And it's not just social media. It's impossible to read the news, watch any video clip, listen to any music, or stay informed about literally anything without having to endure several ads. Every single ad uses up web traffic, electricity, data, and degrades our device performance. And the only people these benefit are those who own the companies that make and sell them.

Of course, advertising is only one sector of the economy. Let's not forget the unfathomable amount of clothing, food, packaging, and other materials that are discarded without full use (or no use at all if they're never purchased). This is not to even mention the fact that most of our electronic devices are actually designed to become useless after only a few years. And we're constantly being manipulated into buying newer and bigger vehicles than we need, eating more food than our bodies require, traveling to "exotic" places to see the kind of nature that no longer exists where we live, and on and on.

None of this will come as a surprise. The modern environmental movement, which has been growing since the 1960s, began in response to these trends. In fact, more recently capitalism has taken on a "green" veneer as global climate change becomes a reality that is harder and harder to deny. But this new "green capitalism" perpetuates the same systematic features of capitalism that contribute to environmental degradation. Consumerism and commodification remain the core tenets under the assumption that we can buy and sell our way out of catastrophe. Not to mention the fact that greenhouse gas emissions continue to rise. Add to this the idea of purchasing carbon and biodiversity credits to offset harmful practices, and we now have a perverse method to commodify the very destruction of nature that these credits claim to protect.

With global emissions still rising, polar ice

caps melting, hurricanes strengthening, droughts and floods worsening, and new diseases spreading, it's never been clearer that we simply cannot continue to do things this way. The point here is not to point out how depressing our capitalist system is (although that's certainly the case), but to emphasize the structural and resultant factors that Ecosocialism is in complete and total contrast with. With that opposition in mind, we can now ask the real question.

What Is Ecosocialism?

At its core, Ecosocialism is about making socialism ecological, and making ecology socialist.[5] The point is intentionally twofold. As I mentioned above, much of socialist history has been preoccupied with a productivist logic that has largely disregarded ecological principles. Similarly, ecology (both as an environmental outlook and a scientific discipline) has failed to recognize that the role of capitalism's never-ending quest for wealth accumulation in the destruction of ecosystems and the degradation of the ecosphere in general. Thus, Ecosocialism infuses the class analysis of socialism with the environmental analysis of ecology, and vice versa.

The primary focus of Ecosocialism is on production. That is, the ways in which we produce the goods and services we need to survive, reproduce, and maintain society. The theory is based on the premise that the effects of capitalist production and consumption are unsustainable for both the planet and our species (along with many others). What this means, is that Ecosocialism presents a new way to organize the planned production of the goods and services we rely on.

This new form of Ecosocialist production has several fundamental requirements. The first is that it must be democratic. Society itself, not occasionally elected bureaucrats, needs to collectively and cooperatively decide on how and what to produce. This democratic decision-making must exist across all scales of society, from the local to the international. In this sense, Ecosocialism overlaps well with Bookchin's theory of social ecology.

The next requirements are that these decisions should be guided by both an equitable distribution of produced goods and also limiting the ecological impacts of production. Lastly, Ecosocialism requires decisions on what *not to produce*. Advertising is one such sector of the economy, as discussed, that could be dramatically reduced, or even entirely eliminated. Add industrialized warfare to that list, and ceasing those two things alone would drastically improve conditions for society and the planet. More than this, though, a planned ecosocialist economy would seek to democratically eliminate as much waste from production as possible, and in turn would allow for the sustainable management of the ecosystems we depend on. And again, if this sounds familiar, it's because it shares many of the same ideas with the concepts of Democratic Municipalism, Degrowth Communism, and a Dialectically Ecological society which I discussed previously.

There are certainly still many things modern society depends on that would need to be produced in rational, ecological ways. Accomplishing this will take more than just a re-organization of production but also implementing technology in explicitly ecosocialist ways. This doesn't mean we can simply wait for capitalist "innovation" to develop a new technology that will magically repair our relationship with the ecosphere, because this will never happen.

There is nothing inherently capitalist or ecosocialist about any technology, rather what gives technology these characteristics is the economic systems in which technologies are deployed. Technology, along with all the other means of production, must be collectively owned and operated by society. In addition, an ecosocialist technology must be compatible with the goals of ecosocialism, meaning that solar panels, wind turbines, computerized automation, electric vehicles, and other potentially useful technologies must have the goal of increasing social equality and ecological health, not furthering capitalist wealth accumulation.

Ultimately, Ecosocialism is about re-structuring the ways we meet society's needs in equitable ways that preserve and enhance biodiversity and ecosystem functioning.

What Ecosocialism Could Look Like

One of the most difficult questions for socialist visions of society, but also one of the most often asked, is what it would look like to actually look like to make these changes. The reason it's so difficult to answer this is that it's impossible to predict the trajectory that the future will actually take, and if an ecosocialist society does emerge it may not look anything like what we've envisioned. That said, we can still make some theoretical guesses based on the frameworks previously outlined, while acknowledging that the specific forms these take may differ.

We know right away that several primary sectors of the economy would need to change. In Victor Wallis's book on Ecosocialism, *Red-Green Revolution*, he first highlights the agriculture, forestry, and fisheries sector.[6] Under an economic system that doesn't require production for the sake of production, we could implement mixed crop agricultural systems that are less reliant on chemical fertilizers and pesticides. Without an advertising industry manipulating us to consume enormous amounts of beef, we could also reduce beef livestock-raising, which is the unhealthiest, most environmentally destructive, and inefficient form of protein. This would also allow us to conserve more forestland, and eliminating wasteful industries like advertising would in turn lower the demand for forest products, allowing us to manage forests as holistic ecosystems. Similarly, more sustainable methods for the fishing industry could emerge that don't deplete nature fish populations, once the profit-motive is removed. Across all these industries, continually reducing food waste would regularly improve our management of these ecosystems.

Of course, other sectors of the economy would be transformed as well. Public transportation would be heavily subsidized and electrified, without relentless pressure from the automotive industry to prioritize car infrastructure. This would in turn allow for more greenspace, urban gardens, parks, and other public spaces in cities. Energy production would transition to completely renewable sources, facilitated by the much-reduced energy requirements after eliminating wasteful consumption. Automation technology would be put to actually useful tasks that save us time and resources, rather than taking jobs or for the creative tasks we actually enjoy, like the capitalists are attempting to do with AI language and image generators. Education could be free, and encouraged as a lifelong activity toward self-development, rather than a training ground for creating more workers. And lastly, all of this could be paid for multiple times over by simply eliminating the wasteful and devastating industrial military industries.

How We Get There

Like Democratic Municipalism, all of this sounds utopian, and to some extent it is, because we need to envision a better society in order to make one, but perhaps the biggest question of all is how we get there. It's not a question I can fully answer in this book, but the simple answer for now is that we need a movement. We need to convince the mass of the population that not only is there a better way to structure society but also emphasize the specific ways in which this society would be better for them, personally.

Intersectionality is a key approach to identifying the ways our current global capitalist system causes class disparities among different racial, gender, sexuality, and disability identities and communities.[7] Similarly, while climate change is a global issue, its ecological consequences don't manifest equally across space, demographics, class, or identities. The way to build a mass movement is to highlight the specific ways that capitalism and ecological destruction overlap to impact working class people, marginalized races, oppressed genders and sexualities, and those with disabilities.[8]

The challenge, and promise, of this task is that it involves nearly everyone in society. In fact, the only people the current system is working for are the capitalist owners and corporations. The rest of us are left to deal with the poverty, environmental degradation, racism, misogyny, homophobia, and other societal ills that capitalism perpetuates.[9] Once we start to raise our collective consciousness, we begin to see that all of us are in this fight together, and that there is enormous strength in numbers. That is the mass movement we need in order to realize an Ecosocialist future, one in which all members of society have a say on what our relationship to the ecosphere should be.

Conclusion

The premise of the theory is that the waste and environmental destruction of capitalism is unsustainable. We're seeing the evidence of this in the form of worsening hurricanes, floods, droughts, wildfires, and disease outbreaks; along with the collapse of global biodiversity, the bleaching of coral reefs, the changing of vital air and ocean currents, pollution in Low Earth Orbit, and the rapid buildup of microplastics across all forms of life. It's overwhelmingly conclusive that we cannot continue in this way and expect to survive as a species or civilization.

At the same time, previous and existing attempts of socialism have emphasized production in an effort to compete with capitalism. These approaches have wreaked their own examples of environmental destruction and cannot be relied upon to solve our current ecological and climatological crises.

Therefore, Ecosocialism argues for an ecology that is socialist, and a socialism that is ecological. The theory presents a new form of economic production that is democratic, planned, and guided by the equitable distribution of goods. This means emphasizing the forms of production for necessary goods and de-emphasizing the production of those that are unnecessary. It's easy to see how this theory overlaps with some of those previously discussed, and more explicitly, embodies the principles–overcoming capitalism, decarbonizing production, reforming–that any ecological society must be based on.

PART THREE:

Synergies

THE BI-DIRECTIONALITY OF THE NATURE-SOCIETY THREAD

The foundational premise of this text is that nature and society are inseparable, but distinct, entities. Human society, while certainly a part of nature, at the same time cannot be fully dissolved into it as part of a homogenized whole. Understanding the synergistic relations among the theories I've discussed requires an understanding of the bi-directionality of the nature-society relation.

The first direction from which the dynamic can be approached is that society is inseparable from nature. This requires an examination of the materialist, evolutionary, and dialectical origins of humanity and human society. Humans arose out of non-human nature, and this process also gave rise to human society. These developmental relations are critical to understanding the ways in which society is very much a part of nature, and what the political implications of that are.

The second direction the nature-society dynamic can be approached is from the notion that nature is inseparable from society. This, too, has materialist and dialectical origins. Human labor is what mediates our relationship to the non-human world. We rely on all aspects of non-human nature to produce the goods we need to survive, and we increasingly modify nature in order to produce these goods. In this way, nature itself is produced (in the economic sense) by society. Nature (both human and non-human) is also interpreted by society, in the sense that all knowledge of nature is socially produced and subject to both individual and collective biases. The very concept of nature is, then, a product of society.

The point I want to make in this final chapter is that following the thread of a dialectical nature-society dynamic, from either direction, leads to similar conclusions. The various theories of how to ecologize society converge around three fundamental principles: 1) Overcoming capitalism; 2) Decarbonizing production; and 3) Reforming democracy. These three principles are present, to various degrees, across all the theories I've discussed, and thus provide a through-line that will link theories to each other as well as to methodology and practice.

Society is inseparable from nature

Human society, as we have seen, is a remarkably unique form of nature. But this uniqueness does not remove us from nature, regardless of how alienated from it our current society is. Our origins are firmly within the realm of non-human nature, which requires full consideration to derive the political and ethical implications.

Dialectical Naturalism provides a theoretical grounding for making sense of society's origins within nature.[1] Evolution both produces, and is the product of, organic life's diversity and complexity. Evolutionary development is also a historical process of cumulative changes. Each new species, each new trait, even each new gene, is altered from a previous state. In this way, each current state is the embodiment of past states, carrying a record of past development. This is the dialectical nature of Dialectical Naturalism. Humanity, therefore, is an expression of its own development.

If the question is about how society should be organized, a reasonable thing to do is to look at the conditions that gave rise to human society in the first place. I've already pointed out the diversity and complexity inherent in organic life that allows evolution to occur, but evolution is also participatory, to varying degrees across taxa. As neural capacity increases, organisms develop greater degrees of participation in their own evolutionary pathways via growing consciousness. This capability is expressed in to its greatest extent (so far) in humans, as fully conscious beings who have awareness of themselves as such. The ramifications here are that most reasonable way to organize society is one that emphasizes these characteristics of diversity, complexity, freedom and agency over self-direction. In other words, a fully democratic society that manages its production in ways that enhance non-human biodiversity. This is, in essence, Bookchin's theory of Social Ecology.[2]

Taking these ideas from the abstract to something more concrete, Democratic Municipalism is the theories of Dialectical Naturalism and Social Ecology given political form.[3] The municipal ownership of production, combined with fully participatory and democratic control of political decisions, are the primary tenets. With its emphasis on the municipal scale of governance, Democratic Municipalism presents a politics in which individuals have agency over the structure of society via townhall style political debate and decision-making. This is a representation of the participatory nature of evolution from which society originated, while ensuring that decisions are made in the interest of collective society rather than the destructive practice of capitalist wealth accumulation and state oppression.

Relatedly, Degrowth Communism likewise embodies many of the same principles as Democratic Municipalism. In *Slow Down*, Dr. Kohei Saito outlines five "pllars" of Degrowth Communism.[4] These include: production based on use-values; shortening work hours; abolishing the generalized division of work;

democratizing production; and prioritizing essential work. It's not difficult to see how this overlap with the tenets of Democratic Municipalism. In fact, in his book Saito specifically highlights Bookchin's Democratic Municipalism as a potential manifestation of his Degrowth Communism.

So, by beginning with acknowledging society's origins within nature and following that thread, multiple theories converge in much the same place. What's more is that both Democratic Municipalism and Degrowth Communism exhibit the three fundamental principles of ecologizing society that I outlined earlier (overcoming capitalism, decarbonizing the economy, and democratizing production). Thus, by recognizing that society is inseparable from nature, the synergistic nature of several theories becomes evident, allowing us to link them together in a more illuminating fashion than any single theory has in isolation.

Nature is inseparable from society

If society is inseparable from nature, so too is nature inevitably bound up within society. Human society relies upon, modifies, interprets, and even creates its own nature. In these ways, nature is inseparable from human society. This relational view of the nature-society dynamic has both unique and similar implications to those we have seen.

The premise of dialectical ecology–as characterized by Foster and in the Marxist tradition more broadly–is that society's relationship to nature is mediated through labor.[5] Nature provides the raw materials upon which society relies, but these are rarely in a form that can be readily used. Labor, then, is the action that humans take to transform the material of nature into usable goods, and the value these goods have is derived from both the labor required to make them and the resulting use they have to society. This use is often referred to as the use-value. Capitalism transforms this use-value into an exchange value via the market, where goods are not produced for their use at all, but rather for their value that can be exchanged. This is how capitalism alters the nature-society relationship, from one based on meeting the needs of society by producing things for use, to meeting the needs of wealth accumulation by producing things for exchange. Dialectical ecology identifies this site of production as key to overcoming the capitalist exploitation and destruction of nature.

Mediation of the nature-society relationship has a deeper implication than simply producing goods. Labor alters nature. In agriculture, we selectively bred crops for centuries, producing varieties and hybrids that brought higher yields. In forestry, we discovered management techniques that produce more timber. We've developed new methods for mineral, metal and fossil fuel extraction. We've learned to capture solar, wind, water, and geothermal power to produce electricity. In all of these ways and more, human society has altered nature through its labor.

But not only has society altered nature, we

have actually created new natures. Genetic engineering, geo-engineering, vaccines, climate change, synthetic materials, and microplastic accumulation all represent new frontiers of nature that humans have created, whether intentionally or not, for better or for worse.

Nature, therefore, is socially produced.[6] In fact, what we even consider to be (or not) a form of nature is, itself, a social construction. For example, genetic modification through gene splicing technologies like CRISPR are thought by many to be unnatural, while genetic modification of plants and animals has been occurring for millennia via artificial selection. Examining the development of any branch of science reveals the ways in which even the "facts" of science are socially influenced and interpreted through subjective biases. Thus, our entire corpus of knowledge about nature is a social phenomenon.

What this all means is that in recognizing the ways that nature is socially produced, we can identify the structural aspects of society that are degrading the environment and increasingly putting society itself at risk. Ecosocialism identifies the site of production under capitalism as the fundamental structural issue behind our environmental crises.[7] That nature is transformed, altered, and created for exchange value rather than for use-values is the primary source of our distorted nature-society relationship. Of course, as we have seen, Ecosocialism is two-fold. It's not just to make ecological socialist, but to make socialism ecological. Past versions of socialism, such as in the Soviet Union, were in no way immune to ecological catastrophe. Even China, while making incredible strides in transitioning to renewable energy, remains the world's largest emitter of carbon dioxide. These examples reinforce that an authoritative socialism cannot be ecological. It must be democratic and planned from the bottom up in order to fully address the current crises.

In fact, what Ecosocialists like Foster and Garzón Espinosa increasingly call for is planned, Ecosocialist, democratic degrowth.[8] In other words, Degrowth Communism. The unceasing quest for unlimited capitalist growth has put the planet on a path of ecological and climatological catastrophe. Scientists themselves now recognize that leaving the question of how to structure production to market forces is likely to lead to civilizational collapse in the coming centuries. The Ecosocialist solution is democratically planned production based on use-value rather than exchange value. Once more, if this sounds familiar it's because its virtually the same proposition as put forth in Saito's Degrowth Communism and also carries many similarities to Bookchin's Democratic Municipalism. In addition, Ecosocialist degrowth displays the same fundamental principles of overcoming capitalism, decarbonizing production, and reforming democracy that any ecological society must exhibit. Thus, by beginning from the other direction with the premise that society is inseparable from nature, we again end in much the same place as we did in recognizing that nature is inseparable from society.

Conclusion

The point here has been to demonstrate the complimentary and overlapping characteristics that have arisen across decades of ecological and political theorizing. The notion that nature and society are inseparable has led to different strands of theory through which to contemplate how best to reconcile society's current alienation from nature. These separate lines of theory are often isolated from one another, or at times, even antagonistic. And yet, as we've seen, they converge at highly similar visions for creating an ecological society.

That these theories are often not directly in conversation with one another is not evidence of uncertainty. Rather, the fact that each reaches the same conclusion means one singular thing: That creating an ecological society will require overcoming capitalism, decarbonizing production, and reforming democracy.

Furthermore, that a variety of theories lead to this one ultimate conclusion suggests that there is also a variety of ways in which we might achieve an ecological society. While the destination we need to reach may be clear, the way forward is not. For this reason, I believe it is important to spend more time considering the ways that these theories strengthen and complement one another, and less time mired in unproductive theoretical debate. It is quite likely that there are many ways forward, and we should explore and experiment with all of them, using the corresponding theories to guide methodology and praxis.

CROSSTHREADS

If the various theories I've discussed so far can be located along different ends of the nature-society thread, there are some theories that extend across the entire line. These theories provide different forms of critique of the causes of ecological crises, as well as different frameworks and systems of knowledge that while certainly relevant to the previously discussed theories, they're also broader and warrant their own discussion.

Ecofeminism is one such theoretical framework. According to ecofeminist theory, our current ecological and climatological catastrophes originate in our patriarchal and misogynistic form of society. The same structures that perpetuate the oppression of women, as well as queer and trans people, are responsible for the exploitation and destruction of nature. I'll explore these implications more thoroughly in this chapter.

Another distinct but relevant corpus of theory is Traditional Ecological Knowledge. This concept is much broader and perhaps harder to concretely define. It is not a critical theory, by which I mean it does not provide a critique of some aspect of society, but rather it is the name given to the entire body of knowledge developed, preserved, and adapted by traditional and Indigenous cultures. The enormous amount of diversity in the history of human culture makes it difficult to generalize (and in fact, is almost impossible by definition, as we'll see), but it also reflects a diversity of ecological and societal organization that makes it so relevant to the discussion here.

This final chapter examines these two theories that don't fit neatly along the nature-society thread, instead stretching across it in various ways.

Ecofeminism

In *Feminism or Death*, Françoise d'Eaubonne makes one of the earliest cases for an eco-feminism.[1] Writing in the 1970s, she argued that the plight of women and the plight of the planet are one in the same. The patriarchal control of society that oppresses women also exploits the planet's ecological environments on a global scale. The linkages here are complex, and d'Eaubonne's text is not without its controversies, so it's worth taking these two issues one a time before bringing them together.

Western society, for d'Eaubonne, was structurally chauvinistic, misogynistic, patriarchal, and phallically prioritized. The rape and abuse of women (and other genders) were normalized, rationalized, and in some cases, even incentivized. Women did not have control over their bodies nor their economic statuses. While familiar with Marxist class analysis, d'Eaubonne claimed that a larger, more important class divide existed: that between straight men and the rest of the world. And although *Feminism or Death* was originally published half a century ago, much of the situation it describes is equally applicable to today's society. The recent MeToo movement notwithstanding, rape and abuse remain all too prevalent. In fact, the MeToo movement itself was a response to the widespread sexual assault men inflict upon others. Not only that, but at the time of this book's writing (2025) a fascist regime in the United States is aggressively attacking what little gains women have made in abortion and contraceptive access. Ignoring the reactionary objections from J.K. Rowling, queer and gender theory have both advanced considerably since the publishing of d'Eaubonne's text, revealing the similar and unique ways that patriarchal society oppresses the gay, lesbian, and trans communities, in addition to its continual subjugation of cis-gender women.[2] All of this is to say that the plight of those who are not cisgender males has a long history and has improved little to present.

Beyond these societal mistreatments is a more structural exploitation that falls predominately upon women, specifically. This, d'Eaubonne argues, is the expectation to *reproduce* society. The most salient aspect of this is literal reproduction, the act of giving birth. This has clear links to restricted access to abortion and contraceptive mentioned above, as those who can give birth do not have full autonomy over when, how, or why they chose to do so. But the reproduction of society requires more than giving birth. Homes need to be organized, meals cooked, clothes washed, children cared for, dishes cleaned, and so on. Despite employment gains in the workplace, this unpaid labor overwhelmingly falls to women in heterosexual relationships with negative mental, physical, and economic health consequences.[3] This is the plight of women.

What, then, is the plight of the planet? At the time of *Feminism or Death*, it was a situation of rampant pollution. Cities were choking on poor air quality, acid rain was spreading, pesticides and fertilizers were leaching from industrial agriculture, and CO_2 was noticeably rising in the atmosphere. Some of these issues have improved since then; many have not. An unfortunate aspect of d'Eaubonne's argument is that she diagnoses overpopulation as the cause of these problems, and understanding the full implications here requires some careful analysis.

Blaming overpopulation for environmental degradation is an oversimplification of the causes. As discussed throughout the text here, capitalism creates an economic incentive to exploit resources past what is sustainable in a quest for unlimited growth. Ignoring this means ignoring the fact that wealthy, capitalist countries consume far more resources than less wealthy ones, despite often having lower populations and birth rates. Of course, d'Eaubonne was well aware of the destructive nature of capitalism. However, she also was aware of the environmental destruction wrought by the pre-eminent socialist nation of her time, the Soviet Union. As I've discussed, the socialism of the USSR (actually more akin to state capitalism) had its fair share of ecological catastrophes. What d'Eaubonne saw in both nations was a patriarchal structuring of society where women lacked control over their own sexuality and reproduction. This, she argued, was even more the case in less wealthy nations that she claimed were often "backwards" and repressive.

These racist and culturally insensitive characterizations notwithstanding, there *is* a link between capitalism and population. We are seeing this play out presently in the calls from U.S. capitalist class for people to have more children.[4] The simultaneous restrictions to contraceptives and abortion access further align the reactionary, capitalist, and patriarchal elements of society. Capitalists require a larger labor pool to keep the cost of labor low, while the continued oppression of women sustains production itself through unpaid labor and the reproduction of society. These structures allow capitalism to persist, causing more environmental issues as a result. In these ways, d'Eaubonne was not *entirely* incorrect to link the population issue to environmental crises.

The solution is Ecofeminism. More specifically, the version of Ecofeminism that *Feminism or Death* argues for is one in which women cease power, not for the purposes of wielding it, but to eliminate it. Abolishing the structural hierarchies that contribute to the oppression of women would, according to d'Eaubonne, also eliminate the structures that perpetuate ongoing ecological destruction. This bears a strong similarity to Bookchin's Social Ecology, with its roots in anarchism and the elimination of hierarchy. In fact, The Institute of Social Ecology has included courses on Ecofeminism in its curriculum.[5] Through such elimination of structural power and hierarchy we see how Ecofeminism could contribute to a more democratic society, one in which all genders and sexualities have full autonomy over their bodies and lives, and also one in which the sustainability and ecological health of the planet takes priority over exploitative and unnecessary resource extraction for the benefit of the view.

Traditional Ecological Knowledge

Traditional Ecological Knowledge (TEK) is neither a political nor ecological theory. In *Sacred Ecology*, Fikret Berkes defines TEK as, "a cumulative body of knowledge, practice, and belief, evolving by adaptive processes and handed down through generations by cultural transmission, about the relationship of living beings (including humans) with one another and with their environments".[6] Beyond being a collection of knowledge, the cumulative and adaptive characteristics of TEK are of particular importance when understandings its place in broader ecological theory and how it can contribute to a more ecological society in general.

Whether or not TEK constitutes a science as we think of it in Western culture is a matter of historical debate.[7] If we consider science to be part of a wider cultural practice of making sense of the world that all human societies undertake, we can see many similarities. Many traditional and Indigenous cultures have developed sophisticated methods, structures, and institutions for collecting and transmitting the ecological knowledge they obtain. The dynamic, adaptability of TEK aligns with the scientific method's self-correcting mechanisms as well. Knowledge changes over time as new information is gained, analyzed, and put into practice. However, TEK also differs from Western science in important ways. In general, traditional knowledge systems are not just scientific but also have moral and ethical contexts.[8] Thus, there is no separation of nature and culture, or nature and society, in TEK systems. In addition, TEK systems are place-based, location-specific bodies of knowledge. The information developed by traditional cultures is, by definition, ungeneralizable, putting in starker contrast with Western science which is fundamentally reductionist.

Given the long histories of the academic fields

which have examined many TEK systems–human ecology, anthropology, geography, and ethnoecology–it's beyond the scope of this book to highlight the many ways TEK has contributed to Western knowledge. Our understanding of virtually every ecosystem on the planet has been expanded by the knowledge of the Indigenous cultures that have and continue to live in, utilize, and manage it. What is also worth mentioning, is the often-complimentary aspects of TEK to fields of science, particularly those that are interdisciplinary, such as environmental history and environmental ethics.[8] The vast and growing body of literature attests to the value of TEK systems.

Unsurprisingly, the TEK of traditional and Indigenous cultures has also been exploited by Western society. Knowledge of biological resources like medicinal plants and other natural resources have been appropriated by capitalist entities seeking profit, often with little to no benefit to the Indigenous cultures that developed the knowledge required to do so. For this reason, many Indigenous people are starting to organize politically to take greater control over their TEK and the corresponding ecosystems from which that knowledge derived.

What makes TEK most relevant to the theories I've discussed in this book is its contextual basis. Like both Dialectical Ecology and Dialectical Naturalism, TEK does not assume a reductionist, generalizable "law" of nature. Instead, "nature" itself is characterized by specific locations, each with place-based meanings, ethical obligations, and spiritual significance. What's more is that traditional and ecological cultures developed their TEK often over centuries, or even millennia, often learning to manage these ecosystems much more sustainably than Western capitalism has. While certainly not all Indigenous cultures have interacted with their environments in sustainable ways, evidence continues to accumulate around the greater biodiversity and ecosystem functioning of those that they manage.[9]

The extent to which Western society can continue to benefit from TEK depends on both the willingness of Indigenous cultures to share that knowledge (which they are certainly justified in not doing), but also the commitment to responsible use of the knowledge by Western cultures. Capitalism is in no way an adequate economic system for responsible knowledge sharing. Not only is it tied up in the histories of colonialism and settler violence against Indigenous cultures, but it also continues to perpetuate the legacies of that violence today. If we truly want to learn from TEK and apply that knowledge toward making Western society more ecological, we must first recognize and address the exploitative and destructive nature that exists within our society today. That is the only way TEK can contribute to an ecological society.

Conclusion

Both Ecofeminism and Traditional Ecological

Knowledge are relevant to the ways in which we might make society more ecological. Both modes of thought reach across the nature-society thread in separate ways that provide alternative, but important, ways of understanding the current state of the ecosphere.

Ecofeminism reveals the way that the oppression of women is bound up with the exploitative structures in Western society. Whether it's capitalism or an authoritarian "socialism", hierarchy creates the incentives that are wreaking destruction across the planet. The absence of true democracy is coincident with the lack of autonomy that women, queer, and trans people have over their bodies, reproduction, and sexuality. Furthermore, it highlights the need for any ecological society to be intersectional in its intention, recognizing oppression not just in class and gender, but also race. Freedom is a necessity for an ecological society.

Similarly, Traditional Ecological Knowledge provides new ways of thinking about our relationships to our environments. This knowledge, while undoubtedly valuable, need not be given freely by Indigenous societies. And when or if they decide to do so, it must be treated responsibly. Our current economic system provides no mechanism for ethical treatment of cultural knowledge. Should we try to learn from TEK, we must first overcome the logic of capitalism. Doing so will allow us to fully implement sustainable practices with strong records of managing ecosystems to the benefit of humanity while also retaining their inherent complexity and biodiversity. Such should be the true aim of any ecological society.

A CONCLUSION

What This Book Is

As I said previously, there are two purposes for my writing of this book. The first is to collect the ecological and political theories that I believe should form the foundation of any ecological society. And there's never been a more immediate need to transform to such a society. The ecological and climatological threats we currently face are existential. If we are to overcome these threats, then we have to fully understand their causes.

Therefore, this book is a collection of ecological and political theory that diagnose these crises as the result of capitalism and offer the structural understandings required to address it. Production solely for the purpose of exchange-value, private ownership, mechanisms for individual wealth accumulation all contribute to the system that enables environmental destruction.

At the time of this book's writing, Donald Trump is in his second term as president of the United States. He is wielding unprecedented military power against the U.S. public, sending active forces to cities across the country. The state is now fully weaponized against the people, in the interests of capital. These authoritarian, anti-democratic actions will only accelerate global climate change, and without a theoretical basis to explain the resulting environmental degradation we risk sliding into full eco-fascism.

The second purpose of this book is then to connect the different strands of these theories that overlap with each other. If we recognize that society is both distinct and inseparable from nature, then the nature-society dynamic becomes bi-directional. Reconciling this requires following the nature-society thread to its conclusion from each direction. In doing so, the commonalities across political theories become apparent.

I believe that identifying these common ideas is crucial for one simple reason: We do not know how an ecological society will come to be or what form(s) it will take. Many different theoretical ideas can and should contribute to it. The common threads allow different experiments for creating an ecological society to still be guided by fundamental principles. Overcoming capitalism, decarbonizing production, and reforming democracy should, I believe, be this guiding foundation.

This is what I hope to have contributed to with this book. That said, it's also worth clarifying what this book was not meant to achieve.

What This Book Is Not

First, this book is not a how-to guide or recipe for creating an ecological society. As I said previously, it's not clear how an ecological society might manifest from our current one. Many pathways are possible, so any prescriptive instruction would only limit those possibilities. Thus, the text here is meant to serve only as a collection of guiding principles, not a strict set of instructions.

Second, this book does not contain new ecological or political theory. That is by design. The premise of the book, and for the Ecologizing Society project as a whole, is that the knowledge to create an ecological society already exists. We don't need new technology, science, or theory, in order to do so. I do not mean that no new theory is ever needed. Society is always changing and should be examined accordingly, but implementing existing theory, using existing methodology to assess that implementation, and putting existing ideas into practice are more than enough to transform capitalist society into an ecological one. We already have the information we need.

Thirdly, this text is neither an exhaustive list of theory nor a full accounting of those that are presented. The book is not meant for an academic audience. Instead, I wanted to make these theories accessible to a wider audience than that which might typically encounter these ideas. Those who are more familiar with political and ecological theory may take some slight issue with the simplifications I've made here and must extend some leeway in the context of the text's purpose.

Lastly, this book is not a definitive statement. There are as many opinions about these theories as there are people who have studied them. Mine is merely one more on that list. My belief is that a much greater unity among those with anti-capitalist sentiments is needed to overcome the current system. So, I do not want to present my opinions here as the sole, defining view of ecological thought on the left.

What Comes Next

If you're reading this presently to when it was published (2025), then you can look forward to subsequent texts that explore the methodology we can use to create an ecological society, followed by a focus on some practical examples. If you're reading this in the near future, find those texts under Ecologizing Society: Method and Ecologizing Society: Practice. If you're reading this in the far future, hopefully you're already living in an ecological society.

NOTES

An Introduction

1. IPBES (2019) *Global Assessment Report on Biodiversity and Ecosystem Services of the Intergovernmental Science-Policy Platform on Biodiversity and Ecosystem Services.* Brondizio, E.Z, Settele, J., Díaz, S. and Ngo, H.T. (eds). Bonn: IPBES secretariat.
2. *IPCC, (2023) 'Summary for Policymakers.' In Lee, H, and Romero, J. (eds) Climate Change 2023: Synthesis Report. Contribution of Working Groups I, II and III to the Sixth Assessment Report of the Intergovernmental Panel on Climate Change.* Geneva: IPCC, pp. 1-34.
3. Marx, K., (2024). *Theses on feuerbach* (Vol. 3). Minerva Heritage Press.

Dialectical Nature

1. Graeber, D., and Wengrow, D. (2021). *The Dawn*

of Everything: A New History of Humanity. London: Allen Lane.

2. This is to say that humans are biological beings. If culture (and subsequently, society) is the product of human consciousness, then it too has its origins in nature. But while I grant that some highly intelligent species have rudimentary forms of consciousness that we might recognize as giving rise to a kind of simplified culture, so to speak, I am not of the opinion that any other species has a form of consciousness comparable to that of human beings. In other words, we are not separate from nature, but we are distinct.

3. Maybee, J.E., (2016). *Hegel's dialectics.* Standford Encyclopedia of Philosophy

4. Price, A., (2023). *Recovering Bookchin: Social ecology and the crises of our time.* AK Press.

5. Ibid.

6. Ibid.

7. Bookchin, M. (1990/2022) *The Philosophy of Social Ecology: Essays on Dialectical Naturalism.* Chico:AK Press.

8. Fragata, I., Blanckaert, A., Louro, M.A.D., Liberles, D.A. and Bank, C., (2019). *Evolution in the light of fitness landscape theory.* Trends in ecology & evolution, 34(1), pp.69-82.

9. Bookchin, M., (1982). *The ecology of freedom* (p. 232). Naperville: New Dimensions Foundation.

10. Bookchin, M. (1986/2022) *The Modern Crisis.* Chico: AK Press.

11. Ibid.

The Philosophy of Social Ecology

1. Bookchin, M. (1990/2022) *The Philosophy of Social Ecology: Essays on Dialectical Naturalism.* Chico:AK Press.
2. Price, A., (2023). *Recovering Bookchin: Social ecology and the crises of our time.* AK Press.
3. In Stephen J. Gould's *Wonderful Llife* (1981), Gould partially counters this trajectory by arguing that "toward" complexity or diversity. However, Gould also re-enforces Bookchin's broader point about the contingency and contextual nature of evolution.
4. Madhusudhan, N., 2019. *Exoplanetary atmospheres: key insights, challenges, and prospects.* Annual Review of Astronomy and Astrophysics, 57(1), pp.617-663.
5. Bookchin, M., (1982). *The ecology of freedom* (p. 232). Naperville: New Dimensions Foundation.
6. Pew Research Center (2020) *Two-thirds of Americans think government should do more on climate,* Pew Research Center, 23 June.
7. Graeber, D., and Wengrow, D. (2021). *The Dawn of Everything: A New History of Humanity.* London: Allen Lane.
8. Ibid.
9. Zweig, M., (2023). *Class, race, and gender: Challenging the injuries and divisions of*

capitalism. PM Press.

Democratic Municipalism

1. Bookchin, M., (2021). *From urbanization to cities: The politics of democratic municipalism.* AK Press.
2. Bookchin, M., (1982). *The ecology of freedom.* Naperville: New Dimensions Foundation.
3. Táíwò, O.O., (2022). *Elite capture: How the powerful took over identity politics (and everything else).* Haymarket Books.
4. Finley, E. (2025). *Practicing Social Ecology: From Bookchin to Rojava and Beyond.* Pluto Press.
5. By "state" here I am referring to the states within the United States, and using "state" to represent institutions of governance more broadly in the following sentence.

Degrowth Communism

1. Saito, K., (2023). *Marx in the Anthropocene: Towards the idea of degrowth communism.* Cambridge University Press.
2. It's worth pointing out here that there is considerable disagreement around Saito's arguments around the extent to which Marx developed the links between economic growth and his notion of metabolic rift.
3. Saito, K., (2024). *Slow down: The degrowth*

manifesto. Astra Publishing House.
4. Ibid.
5. Parsons, L., (2023). *Carbon colonialism: How rich countries export climate breakdown.* Manchester University Press.
6. Victor, P.A., (2008). *Managing without growth: Slower by design, not disaster. In Managing Without Growth.* Edward Elgar Publishing.
7. Liu, Z., Ciais, P., Deng, Z. et al. (2020). *Near-real-time monitoring of global CO2 emissions reveals the effects of the COVID-19 pandemic.* Nat Commun 11, 5172 https://doi.org/10.1038/s41467-020-18922-7
8. Russell, B., (2019). Beyond the local trap: New municipalism and the rise of the fearless cities. Antipode, 51(3), pp.989-1010.
9. See https://www.fearlesscities.com/en/map [Last accessed on 8 August 2025]

Dialectical Ecology

1. Foster, J.B., (2024). *The Dialectics of Ecology.* Monthly Review Press.
2. Foster, J.B., (2022). *Capitalism in the Anthropocene: Ecological ruin or ecological revolution.* Monthly Review Press.
3. Marx, K., *Capital: Vol.3*
4. Foster, J.B., (2000). *Marx's ecology: Materialism and nature.* Monthly Review Press
5. Ibid.

6. Ibid.
7. Gould, S.J., (1989). *Wonderful life: the Burgess Shale and the nature of history*. WW Norton & Company.
8. The debates around holism, reductionism, essentialism and emergence were and are much more complex and nuanced than Foster lets on. See *The Philosophy of Ecology: From Science to Synthesis* for a more robust accounting the development of ecology as a science (not that these debates are settled currently).
9. Lockwood, B. (2025) *A contextualized ecological theory*. Nature Revews Biodiversity **1**, 213. https://doi.org/10.1038/s44358-025-00034-z
10. Engels, F., *Dialectics of nature*.
11. Moore, J.W. ed., (2016). *Anthropocene or capitalocene?: Nature, history, and the crisis of capitalism*. PM press.
12. Carbon Brief. (2025) Analysis: Record solar growth keeps China's CO2 falling in first half of 2025. Available at: https://www.carbonbrief.org/analysis-record-solar-growth-keeps-chinas-co2-falling-in-first-half-of-2025/ (Accessed: 1 September 2025).

Social Nature

1. Castree, N. and Braun, B., (2001). *Social nature:*

theory, practice and politics. Basil Blackwell Ltd.
2. See https://abcnews.go.com/Technology/scientists-turn-lead-gold-1st-time-split/story?id=121762241 [Last accessed 2 August 2025]
3. Moore, J.W., (2016). The rise of cheap nature.
4. Lockwood, B., (2025). Speculative Ecologies: Anxieties, Hierarchies, and Anarchies in the Natures of Speculative Fiction. Literary Geographies, 11(1), pp.39-54.

Ecosocialism

1. Clark, A., Benoit, P., & Walters, J. (2022). *Government shareholders, wasted resources and climate ambitions: why is China still building new coal-fired power plants?* Climate Policy, 23(1), 25–40. https://doi.org/10.1080/14693062.2022.2062285
2. Löwy, M. (2015). *Ecosocialism: A radical alternative to capitalist catastrophe.* Harmarket Books.
3. Pärssinen, M., Kotila, M., Cuevas, R., Phansalkar, A. and Manner, J., (2018). *Environmental impact assessment of online advertising.* Environmental Impact Assessment Review, 73, pp.177-200.
4. See https://basis.com/blog/digital-advertisings-carbon-footprint-where-do-we-stand-in-2023
5. Löwy, M., (2005). *What is ecosocialism?.*

Capitalism, nature, socialism. 16(2), pp.15-24.
6. Wallis, V., 2023. *Red-Green revolution: The politics and technology of ecosocialism.* Political Animal Press.
7. Táíwò, O.O., (2022). Elite capture: How the powerful took over identity politics (and everything else). Haymarket Books.
8. Táíwò, O.O., 2022. *Reconsidering reparations.* Oxford University Press.
9. d'Eaubonne, F., (2022). *Feminism or Death: How the women's movement can save the planet.* Verso Books.

The Bi-Directionality of the Nature-Society Thread

1. Bookchin, M., (1982). *The ecology of freedom.* Naperville: New Dimensions Foundation.
2. Bookchin, M. (1990/2022) *The Philosophy of Social Ecology: Essays on Dialectical Naturalism.* Chico:AK Press
3. Bookchin, M., (2021). *From urbanization to cities: The politics of democratic municipalism.* AK Press.
4. Saito, K., (2024). *Slow down: The degrowth manifesto.* Astra Publishing House.
5. Foster, J.B., (2024). *The Dialectics of Ecology.* Monthly Review Press.

6. Castree, N. and Braun, B., (2001). *Social nature: theory, practice and politics*. Basil Blackwell Ltd.
7. Löwy, M. (2015). *Ecosocialism: A radical alternative to capitalist catastrophe*. Harmarket Books
8. Garzón Espinosa, A., (2022). *The Limits to Growth: Ecosocialism or Barbarism*. Monthly Review.

CrossThreads

1. d'Eaubonne, F., (2022). *Feminism or Death: How the women's movement can save the planet*. Verso Books.
2. Ibid., xvii-xxxvii
3. Seedat, S. and Rondon, M., (2021). *Women's wellbeing and the burden of unpaid work*. Bmj, 374.
4. Spears, D. and Geruso, M. (2025) *Why Should We Worry About Declining Birth Rates?* Jacobin, 25 July. Available at: https://jacobin.com/2025/07/demography-fertility-population-crisis-longtermism
5. Institute of Social Ecology. (2020) *The history of social ecology*. Available at: https://social-ecology.org/wp/about/history/
6. Berkes, F., (2017). *Sacred ecology*. Routledge. p. 8
7. Bronowski, J., (2008). *The origins of knowledge and imagination*. Yale University Press.

8. Berkes, F., (2017). *Sacred ecology.* Routledge. p. 9

9. Birhanie, A.B., Mengistu, D.A. and Gela, A.G., (2025). *Assessing the carbon sequestration potential of church forest and their implication for climate change mitigation in Jabitehinan District, Ethiopia.* Geo: Geography and Environment, *12*(2), p.e70026.

ACKNOWLEDGME NTS

This project began as the simple idea that we already have all the information we need to make society more ecological. It's also the result of dozens of books, hundreds of cups of coffee, and countless hours of staring at my laptop screen waiting for words to come. Writing is a labor of love and hate, and I genuinely don't know if I could have pushed this across the finish line without the readers of the Brief Ecology newsletter who continually showed support and interest. I'm also indebted to Drew Heiderscheidt for our many conversations about economic theory over beers. I'm grateful to the folks in the Forest Dynamics Lab at Penn State and Centre County DSA for directly and indirectly contributing ideas to this project. Lastly, I'm thankful for my friends and family who have always supported me, and which are too numerous to list here. You know who you are.

Ben Lockwood is an ecologist and geographer at Penn State University and the editor of Brief Ecology.